CLIFTON PARK-HALFMOON PUBLIC LIBRARY

Adrenaline Adventure

Belaying the Line:
Mountain, Rock, and Ice Climbing

Jeff C. Young
ABDO Publishing Company

visit us at
www.abdopublishing.com

Published by ABDO Publishing Company, 8000 West 78th Street, Edina, Minnesota 55439.
Copyright © 2011 by Abdo Consulting Group, Inc. International copyrights reserved in all
countries. No part of this book may be reproduced in any form without written permission from the
publisher. The Checkerboard Library™ is a trademark and logo of ABDO Publishing Company.

Printed in the United States of America, North Mankato, Minnesota.
092010
012011

 PRINTED ON RECYCLED PAPER

Cover Photo: Alamy
Interior Photos: Corbis pp. 22–23, 25; iStockphoto pp. 8, 9, 10, 12, 14, 17, 18, 21, 29, 31;
    Photolibrary pp. 1, 4–5, 7, 10, 11, 13, 15, 17, 27

Series Coordinator: Heidi M.D. Elston
Editors: Heidi M.D. Elston, Megan M. Gunderson, BreAnn Rumsch
Art Direction & Cover Design: Neil Klinepier

Library of Congress Cataloging-in-Publication Data

Young, Jeff C., 1948-
 Belaying the line : mountain, rock, and ice climbing / Jeff C. Young.
   p. cm. -- (Adrenaline adventure)
 ISBN 978-1-61613-547-8
 1. Mountaineering--Juvenile literature. I. Title.
 GV200.Y68 2011
 796.52'2--dc22   0324
                          2010028245

Contents

First Ascents 4

Rock and Ice 6

Climbing Gear 8

Climb Safe 14

Warm-ups 18

How to Climb 20

Competing 22

Famous Climbers 24

How to Start 26

Climb On! 28

Glossary 30

Web Sites 31

Index 32

First Ascents

People have long climbed steep, rocky cliffs. Yet, early climbers attempted these feats only when they had to. Most climbing was done for hunting or to save stranded animals.

Climbing as a sport has a much shorter history. The sport of climbing was born in Europe on August 8, 1786. On that date, Michel-Gabriel Paccard conquered the Mont Blanc summit. This is Europe's highest peak. After that success, climbing's popularity soared.

The Himalayas in Asia are home to some of the world's tallest peaks and toughest climbs. In 1953, Sir Edmund Hillary and **Sherpa** Tenzing Norgay reached the summit of Mount Everest. This is the highest mountain in the world!

The next year, two Italian mountaineers made the first ascent of K2. This is the world's second-highest mountain. Soon, everyone wanted to make first ascents.

Since then, climbers have conquered many more mountains. Different types of climbing have developed.

And, equipment has improved. Most recently, indoor climbing walls, climbing gyms, and bouldering have added to the sport's appeal. Climbers can enjoy the sport all year long, no matter where they live. Today, climbers of all skill levels are seeking adventure indoors and out while belaying the line!

Rock and Ice

Rock climbing is done on both natural formations and artificial climbing walls. Climbers use equipment such as ropes and harnesses. They also create anchors for protection against falls.

Many climbers train for rock climbing by bouldering. Climbers scale large boulders that are only several feet above the ground. They don't use ropes or harnesses. If a climber slips off a boulder, a crash pad cushions the fall. A spotter stands below or behind the climber. The spotter makes sure the falling climber will hit the mat.

Ice climbing is just what its name suggests. Ice climbers ascend ice-covered surfaces such as frozen waterfalls. They use special tools such as ice axes and crampons to scale the icy surfaces.

Today, there are two common methods of mountain climbing. They are alpine style and expedition style. Mountaineers in alpine style climbing carry only the bare essentials. By climbing light and always moving up, they are able to reach the summit quickly.

Bouldering is just as exciting as rock climbing. But, no special equipment is needed. So, it's a great way to break into the sport of climbing!

Expedition style climbing involves setting up a network of stocked camps along the climbing route. Climbers don't have to carry all of their equipment and supplies. They can climb at their own pace. And, they can retreat to lower camps for protection against storms.

7

Climbing Gear

A rope is a climber's lifeline. It keeps the climber secure. Climbing ropes come in a variety of sizes, colors, and types. Rock climbers usually use rope that is 197 feet (60 m) long and 0.43 inches (11 mm) in **diameter**. Ice climbers and alpinists prefer ropes that are smaller and lighter. Or, they use double ropes.

When the rope is not in use, many climbers keep it inside a bag. This protects it from being damaged by dirt and water. A safe climber will always inspect the rope before starting a climb.

Climbers use anchors to secure themselves and the rope along the route. An anchor may be a boulder or a tree. It may also be a device that can be tightly wedged into cracks in the rock. This includes wires, hexes, and cams.

A lot of gear is needed to keep climbers safe! This includes cams, nuts, and quickdraws.

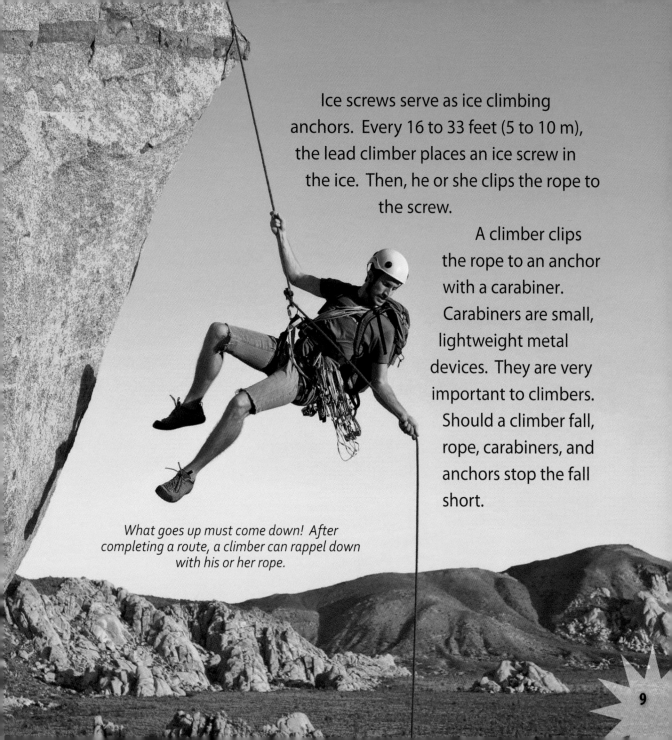

Ice screws serve as ice climbing anchors. Every 16 to 33 feet (5 to 10 m), the lead climber places an ice screw in the ice. Then, he or she clips the rope to the screw.

A climber clips the rope to an anchor with a carabiner. Carabiners are small, lightweight metal devices. They are very important to climbers. Should a climber fall, rope, carabiners, and anchors stop the fall short.

What goes up must come down! After completing a route, a climber can rappel down with his or her rope.

9

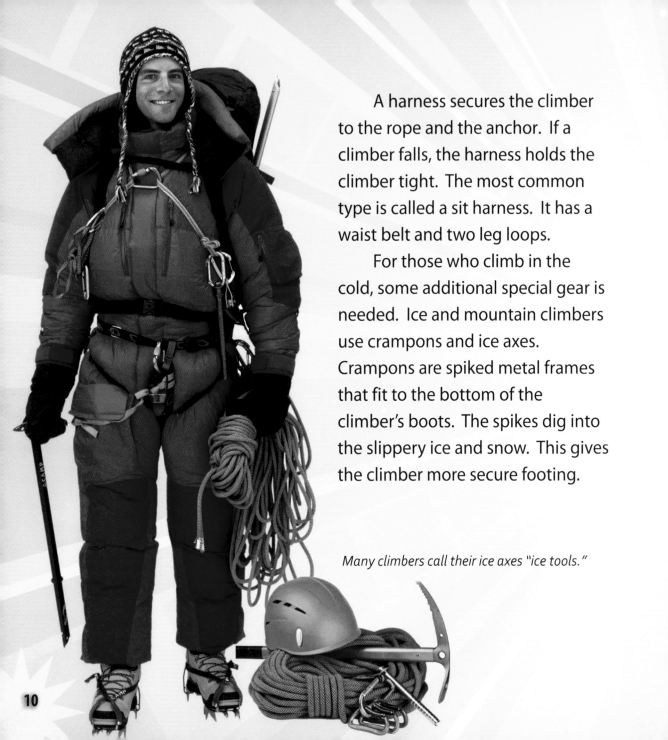

A harness secures the climber to the rope and the anchor. If a climber falls, the harness holds the climber tight. The most common type is called a sit harness. It has a waist belt and two leg loops.

For those who climb in the cold, some additional special gear is needed. Ice and mountain climbers use crampons and ice axes. Crampons are spiked metal frames that fit to the bottom of the climber's boots. The spikes dig into the slippery ice and snow. This gives the climber more secure footing.

Many climbers call their ice axes "ice tools."

Rock shoes increase the grip on a climbing wall or a rock.

Ice axes help climbers in both their ascents and descents. The head of an ice ax has two different ends. The pick is the slightly curved, pointed end used to dig into the ice. The other end may feature a hammer or an adze. Climbers use this end to cut steps and clear away snow. The base of the ice ax has a steel point called a spike. It allows the ax to plunge more easily into snow.

Mountain and ice climbers also need warm clothing. Fleece hats, jackets, and pants provide warmth. Waterproof jackets and pants keep climbers dry. These climbers also need heavy-duty boots that can be used with crampons.

In warmer temperatures, most climbers carry a bag of chalk dust. This helps keep their hands dry while giving them a firmer grip. Rock climbers also need special footwear. Rock climbing shoes should have a snug, tight fit. They are usually made of **flexible** leather and have sticky rubber soles.

Map reading is an important skill for climbing. To stay on course, many climbers use navigational tools. They enter a series of landmarks called waypoints into a GPS receiver. This maps out a route for the climbers to follow. The receiver remembers a series of places the climber traveled through. These are called track points. On the return trip, this keeps the climber on course.

Protect your head from falling rocks and other dangers!

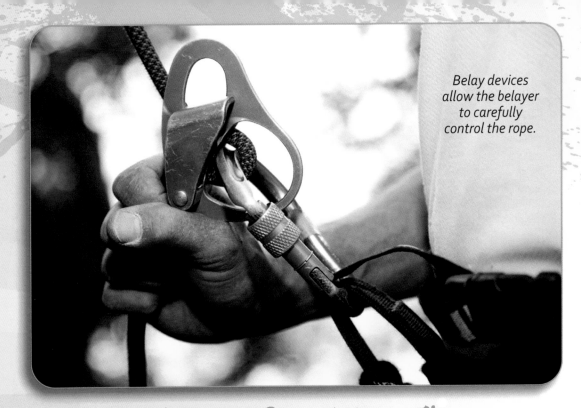

Belay devices allow the belayer to carefully control the rope.

Climb Safe

Climbing requires focus and concentration, as well as steady hands, feet, and nerves. It should not be attempted while under the influence of alcohol or other drugs.

A smart, safe climber will check the weather before starting a climb. Climbing shouldn't be attempted in any type of storm.

Stormy weather brings dangerous conditions such as rain, snow, sleet, hail, and strong winds. Wet snow and rain make rock surfaces slippery.

Before starting any climb, a climber always runs through a series of equipment checks. This includes checking harnesses, knots, ropes, and belay devices. Double-checking keeps them even safer!

Having an experienced belayer also helps keep a climber safe. The belayer feeds the rope to the climber through a belay device attached to his or her harness. The belayer monitors the

For safety, climbers should not climb alone. As you climb, the belayer keeps an eye on you and is there for support.

rope at all times. This keeps the climber from hitting the ground if he or she should fall. The belayer must always pay attention. And, he or she should never take a climber off belay until given permission.

An unexpected fall is always one of the dangers of climbing. If a climber is far from a road or a base camp, this can be especially dangerous. Climbers should travel in groups, carry first aid kits, and carefully plan their routes. They should also tell others their destination and when they plan to return.

Mountain climbers face dangers such as hidden **crevasses**, **avalanches**, hypothermia, and altitude sickness. While traveling along glaciers and snowfields, climbers rope themselves together. If the first climber falls into a crevasse, the second climber can pull him or her out.

Hypothermia is a serious loss of body heat. It affects the body's vital organs, such as the heart and lungs. This in turn affects a person's physical and mental abilities, which can lead to injury. To prevent hypothermia, climbers should stay as dry as possible. They should also drink water, eat, and take frequent breaks.

As altitude increases, oxygen in the air decreases. Everyone's bodies respond to this change differently. Some people experience altitude sickness. **Symptoms** include dizziness, headache, and

shortness of breath. A climber experiencing these **symptoms** should move to a lower altitude immediately. Some expedition climbers use bottled oxygen to help them reach higher heights.

Crampons allow mountaineers and ice climbers to reach new heights! Each style of climbing requires a different type of crampon.

Warm-ups

A beginner should start his or her climbing experience by taking a class. Through experience and practice, a climber's skills will improve. The more you train, the better you will be. You will also gain **confidence** in your skills.

Climbers need to be physically fit. They should have strong arm and leg muscles and **endurance**. Many climbers stay in shape by jogging, hiking, and biking.

Climbing involves a lot of stretching and reaching. So, some climbers do yoga exercises. Yoga requires balance and **flexibility**. Those are qualities a good climber needs.

Yoga also teaches ways of controlling the flow of the breath. This helps climbers stay calm and focused in all kinds of situations.

Before starting any climb, warm up with a few simple exercises. This will help prevent injury. Jumping jacks, walking, skipping, or even running in place will get your blood pumping. Follow that up with some slow stretches to get yourself limber.

Now, focus on slowing down your breathing. Take some deep, steady breaths. Think about your climb and the fun you are going to have. Check your gear. Now you are ready to start your climb!

LINGO

"BELAY ON" – a command used by the belayer to let the lead climber know that he or she is on belay and it is safe to climb.

BINER – an abbreviation of carabiner.

"CLIMB ON" – a command used by the belayer following the climber's "climbing" command. It tells the climber to proceed and the belayer will manage the rope as necessary.

"CLIMBING" – a command used by the climber to let the belayer know he or she is ready to climb.

"FALLING" – what a climber yells to signal that he or she is in a fall.

"OFF BELAY" – a command used by the climber to let the belayer know he or she may remove the belay.

PRO – protection devices such as chocks, hexes, and camming devices that serve as anchors.

PROBLEM – a bouldering route.

"ROCK" – a command used to alert other climbers to falling objects.

"UP ROPE" – a command from the climber asking the belayer to take in the rope's slack.

"WATCH ME" – the climber to the belayer when he or she is nervous or in a difficult spot.

How to Climb

Each style of climbing requires different skills. Top-rope climbing is a good way to get introduced to the sport. Many consider this the safest form of climbing.

When top-rope climbing, the rope is always anchored above the climber. The climber is attached to one end of the rope. His or her partner, the belayer, is at the other end. The belayer keeps the rope tight as the climber ascends the route. He or she stops the rope if the climber falls.

A more technical kind of climbing involves a lead climber and a belayer. The lead climber ascends first. There is no anchor above the leader. Instead, the leader places protection in the rock or ice. Then, he or she clips the rope to the anchors with carabiners. This ensures the climber will never fall to the ground. As the belayer climbs, he or she removes the anchors.

Ice climbers also top-rope and lead climb. They just use special equipment to do these types of climbs. To ascend frozen surfaces,

Top-rope climbing is a good way to learn trust in your gear.

climbers kick the front points of each crampon into the ice. Then, they swing each ice ax into the ice. They pull themselves up and resecure the crampons slightly higher up. Climbers repeat this method to move up the ice.

Competing

Most rock climbers don't engage in competition. They climb for exercise and recreation. Still, some climbers like to see who can climb a route the fastest. Others try conquering the most difficult challenge.

Rock climbing competitions have rules to ensure safety, fair play, and sportsmanship. Most of the rules are concerned with using the proper equipment and correct climbing **techniques**. Yet the rules can vary for each competition.

Speed climbers train hard to be the fastest climbers!

USA Climbing governs U.S. competitions in bouldering, sports climbing, and speed climbing. The International Federation of Sport Climbing (IFSC) oversees international competitions. The three major competitions are in speed climbing, lead climbing, and bouldering.

In speed climbing, time is everything. The fastest climber wins! Lead climbing competitions are all about difficulty. Skilled climbers compete against each other to see who can ascend the highest.

Bouldering competitions involve short routes. Climbers use high-strength, difficult moves to complete a problem. Judges reward points for each completed route.

Famous Climbers

Chris Sharma is considered one of the world's best rock climbers. Sharma started climbing when he was 12. He turned professional when he was 16. Sharma has conquered some of the world's most difficult climbing routes. There are no signs of him slowing down!

Chris Bloch is a world-class speed climber. He is well known for the many medals he has won at the **X Games**. Bloch even has a trading card!

Lisa Rands is one of the world's top female climbers. In June 2002, she became the only American woman to win a bouldering World Cup. She had a second international win the next month. With that, she was ranked number one in the world in competitive bouldering! Rands continues to be an inspiration to women climbers worldwide.

Chris Sharma

As a teenager, Tori Allen made a name for herself in the climbing world. In 2001, she became the youngest climber to summit Yosemite's El Capitan. The next year, she won a gold medal in the **X Games** speed climbing competition. She became the first American woman to achieve this. For Allen, the sky is the limit!

How to Start

Climbing is a sport for all ages. There are many places to learn to climb. There is probably an indoor climbing wall in your area. Check local gyms, sporting goods stores, and fitness clubs. Some also have artificial boulders. They may even offer lessons for beginners. Experienced instructors teach basic **techniques**, use of equipment, and safety practices.

There are two well-known U.S. climbing schools. The National Outdoor Leadership School is in Lander, Wyoming. Garrison, New York, is home to Outward Bound Incorporated. The American Alpine Club can also provide information on other climbing clubs and services.

Research shows there are numerous benefits to regular climbing. These include improved **flexibility**, strength, **cardiovascular** and muscular **endurance**, and mental toughness. You will also gain **confidence** in your climbing skills. In turn, you will have the courage to face other challenges and tests in life.

Climbing is a great way to enjoy nature while sneaking in some exercise!

Climb On!

The United States offers a variety of climbing opportunities for people of all skill levels. Boulder, Colorado, is an excellent climbing destination. California's Yosemite Valley is also popular. However, it is not for beginners. The best-known rock formation there is El Capitan. It rises more than 3,000 feet (900 m) above the valley floor.

There are many great climbing destinations outside of the United States, too. Mount Arapiles in Australia is a well-known and often visited climbing site. It offers something for everyone. In Italy, the steep walls of the Dolomites challenge climbers of all levels. The European Alps offer thousands of climbs. Beginners and experts alike have a variety of routes to choose from.

For American snow and ice climbers, Ouray Ice Park in Colorado is a popular spot. Chamonix, France, is a favored destination for European snow and ice climbers.

It might seem like Mount Everest is a long way from your local climbing wall! But your skill level will improve with practice. Someday, you just might end up bagging the Seven Summits. So find a partner and start belaying the line!

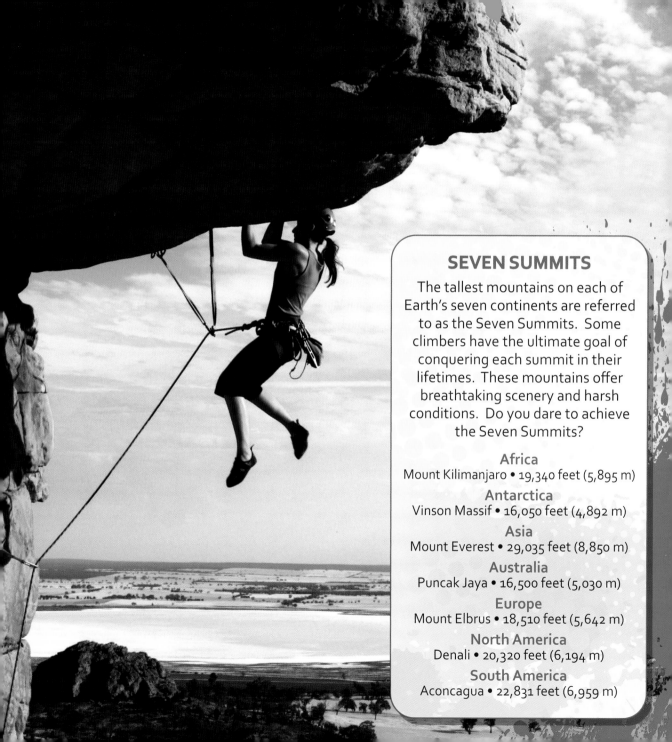

SEVEN SUMMITS

The tallest mountains on each of Earth's seven continents are referred to as the Seven Summits. Some climbers have the ultimate goal of conquering each summit in their lifetimes. These mountains offer breathtaking scenery and harsh conditions. Do you dare to achieve the Seven Summits?

Africa
Mount Kilimanjaro • 19,340 feet (5,895 m)

Antarctica
Vinson Massif • 16,050 feet (4,892 m)

Asia
Mount Everest • 29,035 feet (8,850 m)

Australia
Puncak Jaya • 16,500 feet (5,030 m)

Europe
Mount Elbrus • 18,510 feet (5,642 m)

North America
Denali • 20,320 feet (6,194 m)

South America
Aconcagua • 22,831 feet (6,959 m)

Glossary

avalanche - a large mass of snow, dirt, or other material sliding down a mountainside or over a cliff.

cardiovascular - of, relating to, or involving the heart and blood vessels.

confidence - faith in oneself and one's powers.

crevasse - a deep crack or split in the earth or the ice of a glacier.

diameter - the distance across the middle of an object, such as a circle.

endurance - the ability to sustain a long, stressful effort or activity.

flexible - able to bend or move easily.

Sherpa - a member of a Tibetan people of Nepal. Sherpas have served as guides and porters for most of the expeditions to climb Mount Everest.

symptom - a noticeable change in the normal working of the body. A symptom indicates or accompanies disease, sickness, or other malfunction.

technique - a method or style in which something is done.

X Games - a commercial annual sports event run by ESPN that focuses on extreme action sports.

Web Sites

To learn more about climbing, visit ABDO Publishing Company online. Web sites about climbing are featured on our Book Links page. These links are routinely monitored and updated to provide the most current information available.
www.abdopublishing.com

Index

A

Allen, Tori 25
altitude sickness 16, 17
American Alpine Club 26
anchors 6, 8, 9, 10, 20
Arapiles, Mount 28
Asia 4
Australia 28

B

belay devices 15
belayer 15, 16, 20
Blanc, Mont 4
Bloch, Chris 24

C

carabiners 9, 20
chalk dust 13
clothing 12
competitions 22, 23, 24, 25
crampons 6, 10, 12, 21

E

El Capitan 25, 28
Europe 4, 28
Everest, Mount 4, 28

F

falls 6, 9, 10, 16, 20
footwear 10, 12, 13

G

GPS receiver 13

H

harnesses 6, 10, 15
Hillary, Edmund 4
history 4, 5
hypothermia 16

I

ice axes 6, 10, 12, 21
International Federation of
    Sport Climbing 23

K

K2 4

N

National Outdoor
    Leadership School 26
Norgay, Tenzing 4
North America 25, 26, 28

O

Outward Bound
    Incorporated 26

P

Paccard, Michel-Gabriel 4
professionals 24, 25

R

Rands, Lisa 24
ropes 6, 8, 9, 10, 15, 16, 20

S

safety 6, 7, 8, 9, 10, 14, 15,
    16, 17, 19, 20, 22, 26
Seven Summits 28
Sharma, Chris 24

U

USA Climbing 23

W

weather 7, 14, 15

X

X Games 24, 25